Written and illustrated by Tara Whyte
First Edition. Published in the United Kingdom.
ISBN 978-1-0682012-0-2

From puddles in Henley to
coconuts in Cayman,
join Indra's family as they
trade woolly jumpers for
warm breezes and Sunday
roasts by the sea.
A heartwarming tale of
adventure, belonging
and island life.

Tara Whyte

Indra's Island Life

From River to Reef

To our Indra,
still floating in the stars,
growing quietly, steadily,
in Mummy's belly.
These are the stories we whisper to the wind–
of sailboats and salty sea sprays,
of coconuts and kindness,
of a home between two worlds.
We can't wait to meet you in the sunshine.

Love always,
Mummy & Daddy x

Before we had coconut trees,
we had puddles.
Big ones.
Splashy ones.

The kind that swallowed your socks whole.

We lived in Henley,
where the river
whispered old songs
and the hedges
smelled like
summer rain.

Mummy wore woolly jumpers.

Daddy made tea
and played piano
late into the night.

And Indra?

He was growing in
Mummy's belly —
and on Sundays, we had
roast dinner like it was
a royal event.

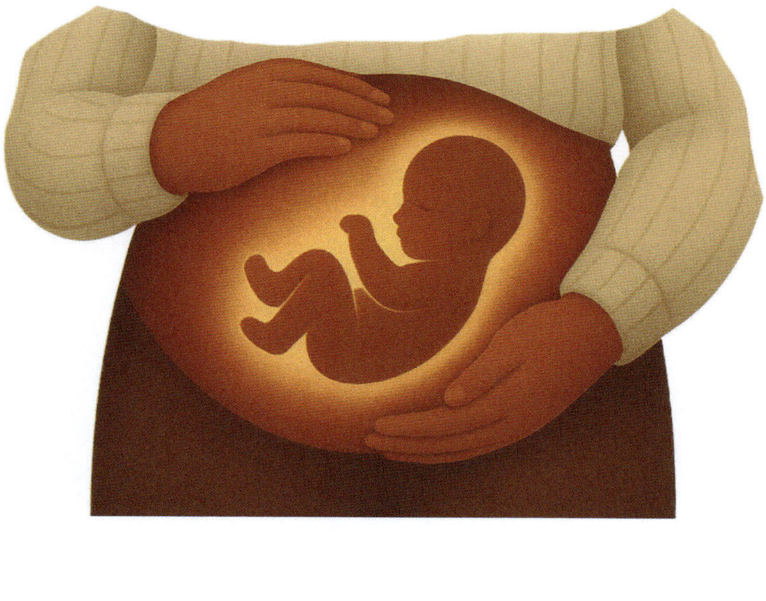

Then one day,
Mummy said...

"Shall we go where the sea is warm and the coconuts fall from trees?

And Daddy
said...

"I'll take the boat out.
You can sit at the front
and look for turtles."

And we just *knew*

Indra would love it

So we flew across the sky to a place called Grand Cayman.

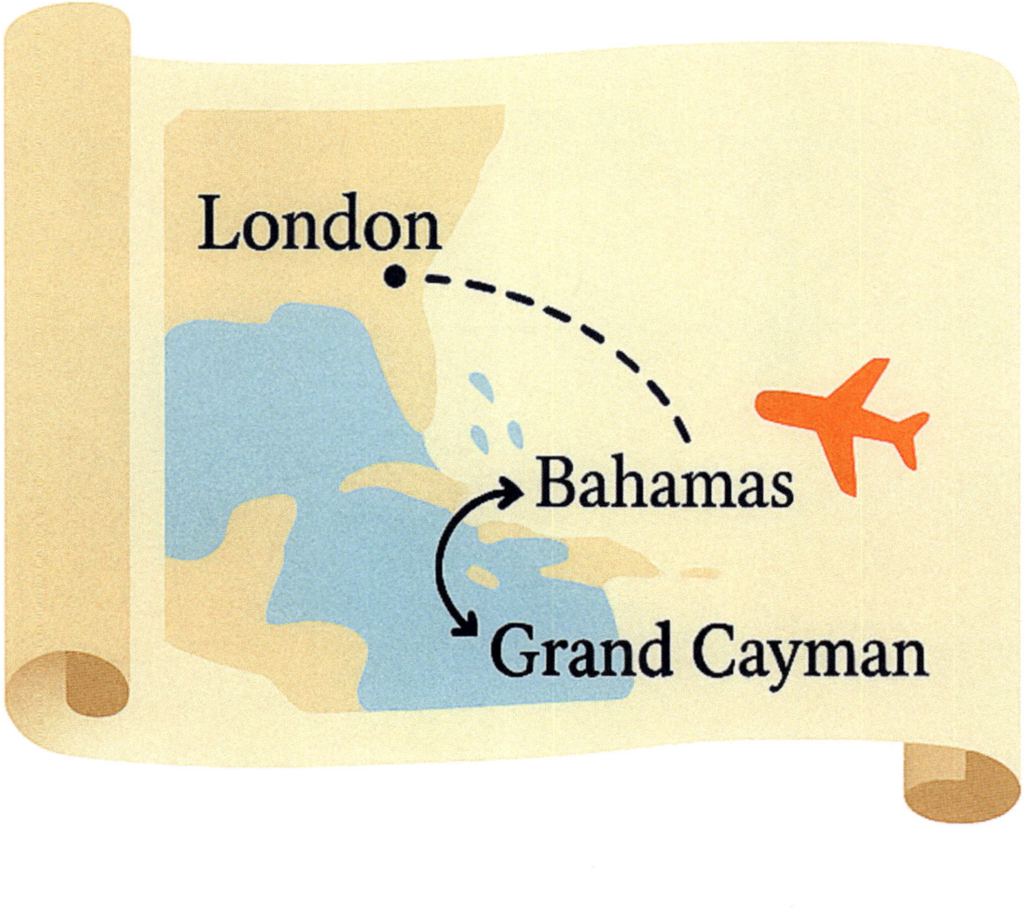

When we stepped off the plane, the sun gave us a big hot hug.

The breeze smelled like mangoes,
and the sand tickled our toes.

Our dream was to
climb trees to
fetch coconuts...

and for Daddy to show
Indra how to slice them open

...to drink the sweet,
milk inside.

We'd snorkel with stingrays that feel like wet silk..

and sail over the
Caribbean ocean,

with the wind
singing our names.

On Saturdays,
we'd stir up
soup—

pumpkin and chocho
bubbling in the pot

while Mummy an Daddy
sing reggae as they cook.

But still, on Sundays,
we make roast dinners–

with gravy, with Yorkshire puds

because even on a tropical
island, there’s something
special about England too.

Now we live between here and there.

Between rivers and reefs.

Between old stories
and new ones we're
writing together.

And wherever
the tide takes us,
Indra should know...

he
belongs.

"Moving with the wind and taking off on a new adventure was a big step for us. Swapping sleepy Henley for tropical horizons taught us that home is not only where the heart is but also where hammocks are.

– Indra's Mummy

Printed in Great Britain
by Amazon

62410890R00022